DEMOCRACY OF FIRE

Also by Susan Cohen

Books

A Different Wakeful Animal
Throat Singing

Chapbooks

Finding the Sweet Spot
Backstroking

Non-Fiction (with Christine Cosgrove)

Normal at Any Cost: Tall Girls, Short Boys, and the Medical Industry's Quest to Manipulate Height

DEMOCRACY

OF

FIRE

SUSAN COHEN

Poems

Broadstone

Library of Congress Control Number 2022943637

ISBN 978-1-956782-18-9

Text & Cover Design by Larry W. Moore
Cover artwork: "The World Is on Fire and It's My Birthday"
Mixed media by Sarah Loyola
Photograph by Valentino Loyola
used by permission

Broadstone Books
An Imprint of
Broadstone Media LLC
418 Ann Street
Frankfort, KY 40601-1929
BroadstoneBooks.com

*Dedicated to my grandparents,
who dared to make the journey*

Contents

III

I

LETTER HOME

I'm staying among strangers. On the shelf, *A History of Finland*.
I spent three days in Helsinki once. When I left, a man saw me off
on the train, made me promise to write, but I couldn't spell his name.

I know nothing about the history of Finland, the way I know nothing
about the strangers I'm living with here, each a country with allegiances
and anthems and alibis. *A History of Finland* makes me think

it is one of many Finnish histories, and possibly not definitive.
My history of Finland has a chapter titled: "Autonomy Lost
and Independence Gained." Could that be us, love?

The Finnish man was a stranger, a blind date the night before.
He took the morning off from work to say goodbye and pressed
his folded future in my palm. To this day I have no idea why.

Maybe he thought I was a country he could live in.
I don't understand what makes people seek each other out.
So many possible histories, so many impossible endings.

I could be speaking Finnish now, farming fish and naming
each of my babies with three k's and too many vowels.
But I'm joined with you, sharing the citizenship of long marriage,

both of us tending our borders. I've never asked if I turned out
to be the person you thought I was, since I'm not the person
I thought I was. I could say you and I will always be

on a blind date—but I don't want to scare you.
When I return home this week, you'll welcome me,
I know, my native land. Love.

Once

People twirled a cat three times and believed
burying it at the crossroads banished warts.
That earth was the matter central to the sun.

That silken-robed angels knew how
to harmonize their harps without lessons.
Masturbation drove men blind,

lobotomy did lunatics a favor,
and a long bath in waters richly blessed
with radium cured almost everything.

My mother believed I had no female wiles.
That I should never beat a boy at ping pong.
That "your daughter's witty, like a man"

was not a compliment, and no prince
would knock at my apartment door
while, inside, I cozied up to shyness.

He rang the bell one day,
a roommate's hometown friend, needing a floor
to crash on until he started grad school.

He was growing his hair long and wearing
what we called a Zapata mustache—
in each fist, a wide-mouthed Mason jar

of his mother's put-up pears
and pickled figs. She'd instructed him:
houseguests must not come empty-handed,

back when a woman's place was in the home
where a woman's work was never done.
Once, a kiss could make you pregnant. *Presto*

change-o, as we said once, love was supposed
to be free. He introduced himself, gazing shyly
past my shoulder. Yeah, I invited him inside.

ANTHROPOMETRY

You and I have traveled here again:
older couple side-by-side at the altar
of art. This time, not Picasso's
fractured female faces arranged
into ugliness, but Yves Klein's abstract
swathes of blue, *Anthropometries*.
He'd plunge a model naked into paint
and drag her across the canvas, his living brush.
I look for any preserved geography of flesh,
some mark of curve or crevice, nipple-prick,
trace left by her dripping pubic wedge of hair.
I see only: His whim. His will. Her willingness.
We are a woman and a man, our heads bent
to the same work of understanding the world.
Still, I have no idea what you are seeing.

CANINE

My friend's husband had always
been a man meager with his words.
Within ten minutes he parceled out
the ones he needed.
The last of the golden retrievers
they liked to keep—whose names
I never could remember—
hugged the floor between us.
Without thinking, I reached down
in the stilted silence to feel the comfort
of its coat, and the retriever rose
and nosed her head onto my knee.
I scratched behind her ears. She snuggled in.
I cupped her face and said,
pretending to be a dog person:
You miss Aleta, too. We were looking
into the black center of each other's eyes
when a sound sirened out of her—
from somewhere dark and deeper
than I ever thought a dog went.
It carried on and on, that sound,
the same moaning wail that,
five years later, still sticks
in the back of my throat.

Bright Clutter

Because I read about space junk and glimpsed that image
of a Tesla, mannequin at the wheel as it shot past Mars,

today I see my nephew floating in the ocean. He travels
as molecules among glittering galaxies of fish,

but I see him back inside his skull, mutely mouthing
underwater. His small plane plunged to the Pacific

years ago, linking what's above with what's below.
Currents spun him round for days. Food for fish.

Matter swallowed by black holes.
He still drifts between the worlds for me, eternal

as a plastic man and occupied with nothing.
It's the ocean that stays busy. I forgive the ocean.

I love to stare at how stubbornly it moves.
Except he keeps washing up against me, stuck

between forever and never again, bright clutter
the universe refuses to erase and no one can retrieve.

MUTED

I'm in the mountains with my holiday heart.
The news seems farther away here, walled off by granite.

I could make a poem from the syntax of gabbro, tufa, schist,
and a coyote slinking past me like someone caught in the wrong bed.

The wind today is ratcheting up, silencing jays
and grounding the swallows I admired yesterday.

Wildness blows off the Sierras: scent of snowmelt
and stone, light reflecting the hungry eyes of bears.

Wind in this valley is like a siren, going and going,
like airplane noise all day at home when a flight path changes.

My son once complained *life is too big for me right now.*
If an ocean is an open question, always reaching for something,

a mountain is a conclusion, a towering end point.
The wind finally bullies me into leaving the deck.

In bed, I curl around whatever heat I brought with me.
Too many stars. I turn mute with moon.

Natural History

It seemed natural to be alive back then—Jack Gilbert

If there is a place where being alive
seems natural, it should be here
in the bright gravity of a mountain,
its hollows still wet with snow in June.
Sunset rouges the clouds.
Somewhere near, a stream
goes about its enterprise.
Wind sizes up some sugar pines
while a bug takes me for natural,
landing to nurse on my salt.
Once, I sat on a ledge above a valley,
faced by an immensity of peaks.
I was alive but momentary,
relieved at the size of my unimportance.
Back then, I mostly sat in cafés
complaining life was hard
when life was hardly anything.
Those friends are gone.
To be somewhere between sky
and dirt seems enough now that death
feels more and more natural.
The mountain is alive tonight, full
of stream sounds and bats. A dog barks.
The spring snow that dazzled me
melts into the dark.

Green Burial

... one of the country's first environmentally conscious green cemeteries...

But rain clawed at the grass,
gouging rivulets,
and the hillside gushed
copper-colored sludge—
a breach in all the greens
around us, like the boulders
placed instead of stars or crosses.

Someone gave us
bamboo staves
so we wouldn't slip
on the steep climb down
to the grave mid-slope,
and warned us not to stand
too near the hand-dug corners.

What a biblical rain
as the sky shook
with trauma, bucketing
so hard we could barely hear
ourselves reciting Kaddish
under a canvas canopy
spilling water down our backs.

Down the hill, greens
too numerous to name
chugged down the flood—
blue-green, yellow-green,
sea-green grasses—fed
by naked bones, so many
un-denominated shades.

The sky kept declaring itself
in charge. One by one,
we dropped white lilies

and pinches of Nantucket sand
onto the plain pine box,
each of us taking care
not to slide into the grave.

I Imagine Myself Grateful

And in the end, dirt-swaddled—
the stringy roots of dandelions,
lady smock, lesser celandine
getting to know me.
No rowboat, no ferryman,
no sickening chop to cross.
Afterbirth is membrane.
What can afterlife be made of?
My family will gather.
The bowl I emptied sits ready
to hold tangerines or car keys.
If it's autumn, wind rouses
semaphores of color to compensate
for the brisk season of dying.
I imagine myself grateful,
the way a storm inspires thanks
when the roof is finally patched,
utility bills paid up, the furnace lit.
At last, I'll go back into the dark,
content never to be cold again,
and take everything with me
that was ever really mine.

I Have a Friend Who Hates Flying

On a plane,
she dug her exquisite nails
into my arm.
I don't understand—
I believe it's better to drop
than ooze
towards death. Better the yank
than the slow drift.
A doctor, who gave me
nearly too much anesthesia
to wake from,
shrugged at me afterwards:
oh well, you walked away
from the proverbial plane crash.
I'm not careless
about living,
but I care more about endings.
I come from a long line of endings,
Jews
with a tolerance for vertigo,
a pedigree of disaster.
My friend thinks of an airplane
as a flying coffin.
I think of birds
who occasionally fall out of the sky.
Little fatalists,
how they leave us
to admire that last image of them
swift and feathered in flight.

Science News: Gene Tweak Can Extend Life 500% (But You Have to Be a Worm)

If you can learn to love the fist of darkness, let it close around you. No human touch, dancing in the rain, light at the end of the tunnel. A simplicity of soil, of foamy loam. Strip down to the basic muscle of survival and let earth with all it brings pass through you. Life extends its linear line. Now, how long is long enough?

Science News: Snakes Had Back Legs for 70 Million Years, Fossil Record Says

Let the record show we all were other, once. In the bone, a nag, a lag, an ache. A phantom-feel. Does the snake, belly scrawling dust, itch to sit up on its haunches? Does it swim through grass, back lit by stars, and sense it once kept an eye on the moon? Ages, then a vantage lost. Let the record show we know: some prospect is no longer within reach.

SCIENCE NEWS: THE MOISTURE IN FINGERPRINTS STRENGTHENS HUMAN TOUCH

Because the hand and mind both grasp, we grab a soup spoon in the dark and know it's not a knife. Our fingers probe for meaning, touch being ancient human language. If you're fluent, you'll understand. Strange, though, how we hold tight to what makes us sweat—not because the world is slippery, but because we are.

ANNIVERSARY

It surfaces today.
That afternoon in Greece, the Aegean
inviting you to leave me on the sand. You climbed into the waves

and disappeared for hours.
Finally, there you were—emerging on a rock,
toweling off, naked, twenty-six and so alive you stood erect.

Eros for passion.
Philia for friendship. *Ludus*
for young, flirtatious play. All ancient Greek for types of love.

If you had floated away
into the topaz forever of that cove,
we'd never have understood the *pragma* of long marriage.

To translate it
as the daily give and take is like
describing any ocean as pacific, the unrelenting suck and thrust

and churn as swells.
Like saying a girl once waited
on an island when, instead, she caught her first glimpse of exile,

stranded
by a foreign sea that seemed to swallow
her husband whole—and with him all the love she might never know.

LOVE IN A YEAR OF EL NIÑO

That almost-forgotten spill of sound:
rain plunking the avocado tree's
broad leaves like piano keys.
The creek that's kept its quiet
through four years of drought
whoops it up, a partygoer
who has torn off his skinny tie.
I keep opening windows to hear.
Let the terrible politicians practice
their terrible politics. So our future
has been kidnapped by the only people
rich enough to pay ransom.
Let astronauts grow the first flower
in space, dream of deserting earth.
It's raining again in California.
Trees and flowers recall how
to stay alive. Birds begin to recollect
their wings from dust. The Sierras
wear fresh snow the way they did
the first morning we said: *marriage*.
Let's hold a wedding. Let's have our kids
all over again. I want to buy a slicker
and a tiny pair of red rubber boots
to restore the coat closet's memories.
Yesterday, a man took his two-year old
into the woods and showed her
wet-forest smells, how to lift her face
to cold rain, how the drops sting
but not like tears. Did I tell you
I remembered that early morning
in a mountain town: an untracked field,
your ratty watch cap, a church bell
sounding as you ducked and scooped snow
to throw back at me? Did I say
out loud this year how much I love you?

They've Discovered Spiders Can Hear Us

The spiders are listening, love.
I tell you this twice because
I still want to astonish you.
I watch you cup a spider in your palm, fling it out onto the soft night.
At least we try to be harmless.
In the sweep of the delicate world you and I are the axe,
cousins to the undertaker.
Our feet pummel ants, grass blades, the living lichen.
Even our voices bother the air,
make a spider above our bed bristle.
The loud speaking of our fingers, your hands on me,
each is a disturbance
when we move apart, when we move together.

When we move apart, when we move together,
each is a disturbance.
The loud speaking of our fingers, your hands on me,
make a spider above our bed bristle.
Even our voices bother the air.
Our feet pummel ants, grass blades, the living lichen,
cousins to the undertaker.
In the sweep of the delicate world you and I are the axe.
At least we try to be harmless.
I watch you cup a spider in your hand, fling it out onto the soft night.
I still want to astonish you.
I tell you this twice because
the spiders are listening, love.

II

THE DRILL

I love having a daughter, grown.
We laugh the same staccato laugh.

She's walking with me in winter sun, past plum trees
whose early bloom survived a recent shock of hail,
the morning not as warm as it looks.

She tugs up her collar, the only person I know
whose eardrums ache just like mine in wind.

Now she's saying she's been told: Don't
unlock your classroom door, even if a child
bangs, terrified, and begs you to let her in.

She teaches her fifth graders to Run, Hide,
Defend—the country's common lesson plan,
the latest in education for mortality.

She's supposed to run with them,
not hang back to shepherd slow ones,
not hover over any child-body
to call out a name without a future.

If they're locked down, she's been told
to grab the red extinguisher, ready
to squelch the fire in his eyes.
Then the boys can tackle him.

Her children practice their assignments:
Lower blinds. Stack chairs and desks
and tables to build a barricade.

We have calm voices, but the same
angry country in our veins.

Now she stops to examine a fig tree in leaf,
wondering out loud why it bears buds,
since the one next to it stands bare as bone.

It seems random—how only some will
get the chance to open.

Report on the State of the World's Children

They took me to sea in a faulty raft.
I couldn't swim but, dead, I could float.

I came from the wrong tribe.
They took me at night over mountains

and let go of my hand. I was born
at the wrong time. They took me to a place

of tents and snow. The heat was fire
and they rationed the flames.

Winter entered to sleep with us,
also men harsher than winter.

I was brave. Only my dreams cried out.
I came from the wrong village.

They took me to a camp with tall fences
cholera could vault.

I crossed from a wrong country.
Alone, I wandered a desert.

I slept under a cactus for weeks,
until crows found me.

They took me to jail. I watched a green fly
who was allowed to come and go.

They pronounced my wrong name.
I prayed the wrong way.

They took my house and gave me rubble,
then told me to go home.

I sat day after day and made walls
from all that I had—my two arms

became *mother* and *father*, holding
each other and hugging my knees.

Photograph of Claudia Patricia Gómez González, Killed by U.S. Border Patrol Agent

Her aunt holds it up, so we can see more colors than brown.
Purple, ruby, and canary-yellow stripe her apron in the photo,
embroidered butterflies with magenta wings
above the orange trumpet flowers on her bodice.
How small she is, nineteen, fists-on-hips, facing forward
towards her lover who wants her to join him in Virginia.
She squints, and fatigue underlines her eyes,
as if her Mayan village offers too much sun
along with too much worry and too little work.
Only the bush behind her prospers, big-leafed and glossy.
She wanted to be an accountant, her aunt tells reporters.
You can't get more American than wanting enough money
to count. Afterwards, a witness described her face—
one side dirt, the other blood—in a junk-strewn lot
less than a mile into Texas. We're told it's wrong
to make a poem from someone else's tragedy,
but she crossed the border and became ours.

EXHILARATION

to my grandparents

Within *exhilarated*: *exile*.
Languages left behind like cloaks.
Your children forgot whole octaves

of your stories. Were you afraid to sing?
Inside *exhilarated*: *hatred* and *tired*.
After your harsh winters, I wish you

a temperate zone to slumber,
hibiscus dreams. Nights, did you sail
backwards in your sleep to villages

of ash, and answer to old names?
I imagine your landings in America.
In *exhilarated* is *exhale*.

ANOTHER ALPHABET

Some letters greet me from childhood
when they wrapped themselves in bearded holiness.

In stiff black coats, they uttered Hebrew and commandments.

Now I'm learning to read Yiddish, and they are somehow rounder.
I chase after them like balloons, unafraid they'll scold me
for running in my dress.

I hope they will become: *daughter, table, green.*
Then *goblet, grapevine, field of rye.*

Maybe *love,* maybe *loneliness.*

I want to cross their borders, press my lips to theirs,
bring them to my ear and listen for their sounds of ocean.

For now, they're *alef, beys, gimel,* and what comes after.

Shlos mem, langer khof, langer fey, langer nun, langer tsadek,
five only used to end a word. Final forms.

An alphabet cannot be dismembered
with a chainsaw in frozen forests outside Vilna,
or slashed to death from horseback near Kiev.

It can be dis-remembered, like a cousin once-removed
who writes a desperate letter.

It can spell *shop* before the shops are shuttered.
It can be *eyes,* then eyes *made closed.*

I'll learn endings later.

I am a beginner, giddy with untested gutturals—
and the alphabet is a woman layered in aprons,
fragrant with baking cinnamon and walnuts.

Her grandchildren cannot understand her,
but they dig into her apron pockets for *rugelach*,
secrets stashed for them to find.

LATER, IN AMERICA

In New Hampshire, my grandmother tried to tell a French-Canadian nurse
they'd wait until the circumcision to name him.

So when my father, Nathan, applied for his first passport, he discovered
he officially began as *Later*. Funny for a man always at the airport early.

His mother's English never prospered.
Her lips would not surrender to its shapes.

She'd been born Yiddish, syllables coating her tongue like milk,
the way first language bears us—sometimes across an ocean.

Yiddish was her Old-New World, where life muttered, shouted, sang,
and begged and wailed and whispered.

When she quizzed her children about their Boston *shul*.
When she mourned the sounds or *klangen* of a *shtetl* street.

Her sons and daughters refused to speak
their American thoughts to her in Yiddish.

I waited too long to ask. Absence cannot answer.
But finally I have learned the words: *far vos?* Why?

Conversation Group in a Haunted Language

April. Ben is always sad.
Troyerik which sounds almost like tragic
which is more than sad. He asks us
for five minutes to describe how his father
and brothers died in the ghetto of *hoongehr*
which sounds almost like hunger but is also
starvation which is more than hunger.
Ben and his mother and the younger children
all still alive until April. Train after train
to camps whose only labor was death.
Yiddish-speaking street after street
after street after street after street
until Poland ran out of its Jews
their plosives their sibilants their ways
of meaning. *We must never forget!*
Judy cries out or maybe it is Millie.
Ben thanks us for listening
his tongue slurry with old age and Warsaw
his watery eyes peering huge
through his glasses like a famished doe's.
Once someone teasingly shushed him and
he slunk into the corner to make us laugh.
Once he shouted a *kuchn is a cake!*
then *breeder-lebn* is *brother-dear close*
like a brother! and made us laugh
at ourselves when translation stumped us.
What will we do without Ben?
Norma asked or maybe Dolores.
He is our library. Today Ben apologizes
for unboxing his archive of sorrow.
He makes his bowlegged way to the door
as if an old weeping softened his bones.
People on the California street take
their everyday steps beside dogwoods
that strew their paths with white petals
as always in April.

Science News: As Animals and Plants Go Extinct, Languages Die Off Too

Inside *languages*: a *lung* and its *lunge* for breath, the way the mind can *gun* the tongue. I wonder how the fox, how the dog, how the doe, complete their thoughts. How god speaks with *angels*, or eagles with their gods. Inside: a *gauge*, an *age*. *Lens*: How the mind sees. *Angle*: How the tongue twists. The way some *sang*, and their last worlds were *sung*.

SCIENCE NEWS: DOGS WERE DOMESTICATED ONCE FROM A LOST POPULATION OF WOLVES

Old friend, chowing down your easy supper, dream-twitching on your doggy bed, better if you had bared your teeth, cornered and devoured us early, before we swallowed forests, ripped the flesh off mountains, bloodied earth entire. Better if you'd domesticated us before we turned into this lost population of wolves.

Science News: Dung Beetles Navigate by Storing Star Maps in their Brains

I ached to teach them how to navigate. I read news to them about the emerging science of emotions. I wrote in a poem, *I have no answers for my children*, when I should have said: Oh, my little beetles, learn to dance on the dung heap and practice your cartography. You might discover you were born knowing how to steer—by sun or moon—through hazardous geographies.

#SARDINIANSUNDAY

My son posts a selfie of his arm reaching for a bottle of beer.
He's floating in the azure, and his Corona floats beside him,
cradled by an inflatable pink flamingo supplied by the resort.
Tattooed on his forearm is the Mayan number eighteen—
Mayan number, because that's the kind of curious math-child
he was, and eighteen because it's the Hebrew symbol for life.
I told him it looked like a bar code, but only because
I tried not to say it made me see him numbered
and skeletal—his mathematical brain and galloping heart
prized only as ash. In the photograph he hash-tagged
practicingmyMichelangelo, he poses his graceful hand
toward the bottle like Adam reaching toward God.
I picture the Mediterranean, the cove's innocent blue
and soft suck, and I want not to say to him: children
are floating face-down in that sea. I want not to imagine
what the water washes without washing away.
How much pleasure are we allowed in one life?
I click "like," then change it to "love."
Our children all float in the same sea. True or false?

Rosh Hashanah with Crow

The crow who made me swerve
stood in the street, peeling the dried fruit of a carcass.
It could have killed me with its gift for prophecy—
foreseeing I'd steer around it into traffic and back, seconds
before it merged with the blackness of my tires.
It would not let go of the string, crow feet
adamant and planted like a tyrant's.

In my rearview mirror, the bird remained
alive and bent in conversation with oblivion, tearing
at whatever grease was hardened on the pavement.
I drove glancing backwards
at how the crow kept bowing to the spread on its altar.
Do I ever abandon myself to any appetite so completely
that I forget to listen for the rumble of disaster?

This was Rosh Hashanah, a day to be written
once again in the book of life, with its running addendum
of casualties. A day to dip into the honey,
but no one in my family was close enough to share it
except by text: *l'shanah tovah* across cities and continents.
How I wanted someone near me to celebrate
our mutual survival: mine, and the crow, and the Jews.

Circuit of Sadness

You don't need an electrician to tell you
        the circuit-breaker board is fried
when you've heard the sizzle,
        gagged on the smoke,
and every lamp in your house refuses
        to obey its switch—

the way you don't need a brain scientist
        to announce he has discovered
and named the *circuit of sadness*
        if you've plugged into that socket
of sorrow and let its current carry you
        round and round, again and again.

When you practice your losses until perfect,
        even before they are lost,
who needs to imagine an eponymous spot
        where emotion and memory slow-dance,
clinging as they rock back and forth
        between amygdala and hippocampus.

You've swept the sawdust path at the circus
        where elephants plod head-down
to nowhere. You've mastered the loop trail
        on that mountain of misery
where Sisyphus pushes uphill
        under skies grayer than grease.

You don't need any expert to plot
        your revolutions of regret,
or pinpoint where it is you dwell
        when you are dwelling—
or count how many times a month you
        drop in as if it's home. No.

You just want someone good with wiring
            to fix it, so lightbulbs resume
their glow and appliances their companionable
            humming—to lift the blackout
and reconnect you—quick, before all those
            sad fish in your freezer thaw.

LOVE IN A YEAR OF OUTRAGE

When you shouted *there it is!*—
like a spiritual awakening—
I ran to see, expecting
I don't know what, maybe
the wedding ring you lost our first year,
an alien ship, or some extinct beast
big-footing it up the drive.
It was dusk and cold and the most
hyperbolic of times. This land
that called out to my ancestors felt so foreign
I thought I should dig up my dead and move.
It was the end of a day, but felt
like the End of Days. You stood
at the French doors facing the dunes,
and peering through binoculars, eager
for me to look up from my dread
to see whatever it was you saw.
In a notch about two inches above the horizon
and sinking fast, the planet Mercury—
a small, golden point
I never would have noticed without you.
The planets continue to hold,
three of them visible last night: Mercury
aglow, reddish Mars, and Venus constant
in our evenings. We are changed.
Yet we're not. I don't know another way
to say it better than how Mercury says it,
remaining where it should, predictable
in the best of ways, exuding the warm color of gold
worn on the hand for a long time, a pinprick ablaze
for longer than our species will exist,
living its only life as light. Between us
and it, there's a distance far beyond air,
and beyond despair.

Yiddish Cento*

It is always about bread and death.
A person can forget everything but eating.
Better an egg today than an ox tomorrow.
Better one friend with a dish of food than a hundred with a sigh.

He who has not tasted the bitter does not understand the sweet.
All is not butter that comes from a cow.
Only in dreams are carrots as big as bears.
If you can't endure the bad, you will not live to witness the good.

A man should stay alive if only out of curiosity.
He should laugh with the lizards.
Laughter is heard farther than weeping.
If you are fated to drown, you will drown in a spoonful of water.

Man begins in dust and ends in dust—
meanwhile, it's good to drink some vodka.
Enjoy life—you can always commit suicide later.
If you're going to eat pork, get it all over your beard.

*all the lines in this poem are Yiddish sayings

Weather Forecast

Later on, besides civic grief, he also began falling into champagne...
—Dostoevsky

Morning will buckle
its marine layer,
its predictable cloud belt.
You'll try to sidle up to words,
barefoot and in pajamas.
Listening to Bach, you'll believe
everything the cello says
about regret. You'll read the news
and adorn yourself with civic grief,
those tattered garlands.
Chances are good the cosmic gears
will grind morning into afternoon
before you notice. Some sun
might just break the skin of fog.
Your lover will come home.
You'll roast a chicken and forget
to be sad. The night will offer
its wine-flavored promises.

III

A Dictionary Names the Wind in the Trees

Psithurism because
what else would we call sound embedded
with leaf mold and breath
zithering just below the daily drone
of power saws and chippers,
eons of air shifting
like an old Chevy through leaves,
riffling papery corn fields
and the eucalyptus,
stuttering through windbreaks,
jittering an aspen
in a beam of breath,
lisping *nothing pins me down*
in the language of the Huron,
in Olmec, in Sanskrit, chittering
all its unpronounceable names,
its tunes with the shiver of pine needles
and the moves of a river?
Psithurism comes as close
to the clash of wind and trees
as *orgasm* comes to the friction
of muscles, nerves, bodies,
which is to say when so many words
cannot catch it,
those of us always searching
for just the right one may
as well stop speaking
and lift our heads
like mule deer, ears twitched
for the smallest sound.

Ephemera

May we learn to market benevolence instead of greed.
May the oceans never suffer silence.

Let us not sacrifice the earth to give the laptop
eternal life. If I forgive vultures their terrible tasks,

will they forgive us ours? May our horizons enlarge
to include both the elephant and its future.

May those glittering mysteries we call galaxies
continue to be preserved from us.

Let the ephemeral stream in my yard
resume its intermittent running—

I can believe in it at all times, unlike gods.
I can never make the invisible appear

unless it is my lap as I sit in the grass.
This ant and beetle on my leg, I overlook

their creepiness, long may they multiply!
May we notice what is visible while it is here

and see what is ephemeral—

the way my lap briefly opens to the beetle
like an endangered landscape

and to the ant, a planet it's been loaned
to walk across softly.

WHERE WILL YOU GO WHEN THINGS GET WORSE?

Surf keeps overwhelming the remains
of a fishing boat beached and abandoned
weeks ago, rubbing it to extinction
wave by wave, plank by plank.
I joke *this must be the ship of state*—
humor being a vehicle for escape.
If you're an astronaut, you can seek
another planet for atmosphere.
If you're a wordsmith,
you can keep hammering, or else
stop and pour the single malt
to shake you nightly off your axis.
I watch sanderlings, tiny birds
who feed on tides—somehow unscathed
by pounding—and I imagine flight.
But once launched, what Arctic
would I land in that isn't melting?
At my feet, red carcasses of crabs,
a shell being another vehicle
that will take you only so far.
If you're a crab, you can swim
or scuttle, or hunker down
on your unsettled patch of sand,
all ten legs braced to resist.

PHOTOSYNTHESIS

—the CDC reportedly bans seven words

Another evidence-based day.
Not a unicorn in the sky.
I pass under a maple's diversity
of red, yellow, orange and brown.
Even with good intentions and a strong
work ethic, leaves are born vulnerable,
death being the one entitlement
of every living thing from blossom
to boy, from fetus to father.
This poem is transgender, meaning
surface is one thing but essence
another. It is not about trees.
We've been advised to swap words
for lies so reality will disappear.
I repeat: *vulnerable, entitlement,*
diversity, transgender, fetus,
but this maple keeps absorbing
the *evidence-based* sun
to produce *science-based* growth.
Remember photosynthesis?
Soon, someone will insist we
just call it magic so we forget
how life depends on light.

To Translate an Idiom

Es vert mir finster in di oygn.—Yiddish saying
It is becoming for me dark in the eyes.

In my eyes *It*
becomes brown tints, black holes, a view

of deer who trot
up the middle of my street, hooves

against pavement.
It becomes the large past and small present,

this late summer
doe who tastes disappearance in a leaf,

the brilliant shine
of any afternoon that turns black with passing.

Isn't light
the universal question? What does *it* mean—

in a syntax
of transitive souls, imperfect verbs?

I see the darkness grow around me.
Or, possibly: *I turn dark inside.*

BREATHING FIRE FROM PARADISE

Muffled sun, mutant air.

I forge a treaty with flames:
Take them—

This chair still solid under me.
This oak table stained with memory.
This picture my daughter painted,
its oils ready. The wall where it hangs.

But let me go,
or let me go quickly.

Breath scratches the back of my throat,
tastes like cigarettes and cinders.
On the wall, a sepia photo of Hopis
who circle a bonfire, wood whispering
its smoke into clouds as they dance.

I pretend smoke-clouds are holy.

The altar isn't empty.

The dead don't swim into my lungs
with each breath.

Trees around me won't gather
their ghosts inside them—

Cedars, maple, birch, and bay laurel,
thick with thirst—

preparing escapes into air.

Science News: A Wild Bird Leads People to Honey

African hive, hot with bees. A man with a stick calls through his teeth; the bird comes, honeyguide. It finds a hive, up where a man can't see, and the man lights his stick to shove smoke into air. Tree, axed. Hive, smashed—spilling its frenzy. This is where the sweetness starts. Pond of syrup, meaty wax. Open for the bird who learned to be called, the man trained by a bird to share.

Science News: Amphibians Glow. Humans Just Couldn't See It—Until Now

Someone thought to shine a blue light, and discovered brilliance on a tiger salamander's back. Gobs of green. Marbled salamander, Cranwell's horned frog, newt with neon stripes. Their beauty dulled by limitations of the human eye. Possibly such flare serves to unnerve their predators. Silly newts. Don't they know how much we cannot see, and yet we stomp everywhere.

SCIENCE NEWS: THE BUBBLE AROUND THE UNIVERSE IS SHAPED LIKE A COLLAPSED CROISSANT

My face in the mirror's oval is the only stranger I'll see today. That's about the shape of things. Each day inside my house: rectangular. Nights go round. A red sunset smears itself flat over the final day of a shapeless year. Let forward be a shape. Also, tomorrow. Hope, like the bubble around the universe, is difficult to draw.

OMENS BEING BAD

The teapot lost its whistle.
Outside, people didn't even try to sing.

Sun struggled to rise before noon,
crouched behind a mask of fog.

Fear kept writing the same lines.

Three-hundred thousand.
Five-hundred thousand.

I couldn't make the numbers add up.

In the same week, two long snakes
paused across dirt trails in front of me.

Both times, I froze and scanned for rattles
while the snakes waited to read the signs

from my jumpy feet. When paths cross
now, we stand apart, trying to divine

which one of us might bode bad luck.
So far, no one I know.

In Greenland the Ice Sheet

is pooling like tears
into the ocean
while we are too busy
planting the fossil beds with our own bones
interred without ceremony.
When people die with no one to hold their hands
how can we be expected to mark the end of an ice sheet
that melted so fast—suddenly
beyond saving.
We have a surfeit of endings
we cannot take in our arms, griefs
we dare not sing in congregation.
We are the sled dogs who slog along tracks,
knee deep in new ice-melt,
head-down and flooded with mourning.
All along we mistook a slippery future
for something we could walk across, the solid form of water
until it began spilling
its dirges into the rhythm of waves.
Meanwhile, the gravitational field shifts over Greenland,
glaciers become waters
and oceans become troughs for the water's dead weight.
Seas rise up and our children are stranded
in their one time to live,
the way polar bears swim now
with no place to go, exhausted
as we are.

Hoop After Hoop

If not for the orcas,
the sea lions would not be leaping
out of their silky wet skins,
wouldn't hurtle towards shore
arcing like dolphins. If our mouths
were not masked, our excitement
would be un-muffled—as stranger
calls out to stranger and points
at the hundreds of slicked bodies
in synchronized panic. December,
but crowds are strung along cliff tops.
We want sharpened air to startle
our lungs into opening wider.
If not for a few spumes like sparklers
at the horizon, no one would know
there were orcas pursuing death coldly,
as the sea lions make for bare rock
to haul out and huddle. Watching them
jump in waves through the waves,
like a troupe performing with brilliance
while the ocean holds up hoop after hoop,
we could think this simply was joy.

In Respect to the Jellyfish

Because we occupy the wrong animal—don't you too feel it?
—Lucia Perillo

Even the gelatinous—moon jellies, giant jellies,
sea gooseberries, and by-the-wind sailors that litter
the beach—have lived their animal lives

and left a shiny trace that lasts only for a while.
Like our own dead, some are still capable of stinging.
I step carefully as I look through them, their jellied

bodies melting into gleam on the sand as if they have
never known where they end and the world begins.
So they dangle in the ocean with a certain uncertainty

at the edges, empty in their fullness and filled
by their emptiness. Why wouldn't I be content to float
day and night, to let my ambivalence take the form

of water shoving me this way and that? To need
no protection of bone and leave no fossil,
living without architecture, outside of history.

To Thee I Sing

for A. J. E.

On your day of birth, America danced with fire. Yes, torches
lit your way, streets flash-banged their salutations.

You who sleep now, plump and swaddled, will grow tall,
a man whose skin may speak of English or Viking

or African blood, whose beard may bush out black or red.
Your first name, picked only for its clink against your last,

is a revenant, echo out of Tangipahoa Parish
and your great-great-grandfather, white son of a slaveholder.

Some of your other greats (names unknown to us)
stepped into this new world as property. Which corpuscles

descend from owners, which from the owned, as they pump
through your singular heart? Which eyelash, which fist?

In an airport someday, you will be asked who you are
and be required to answer. Nationality: American.

Place of birth: Portland, Oregon, while it was in a state
of fury. Your father cradled you home

in the safety of a car seat through a patrolled city.
Virus-plundered, closed by curfew.

If you need to hear such stories, we can sing a lullaby
about this day of shattering and the violent joy you brought.

Welcome! O citizen, born under these unfixed stars
and stripes, you are our nation now.

Just When

After I choose a rock mid-way down the slope
and sit to watch the ocean, a red-tailed hawk
claims the rock below, observes the way
I eat my apple, scans the cliff-side vetch
and wort, launches, pounces on an insect,
then retakes its boulder. I'm used to being
the only hungry predator here, but the hawk
does not seem bothered. It lets me admire
its hook of beak, the holstered power
in its folded wings, its outsized claws
resting on the lichen like scythes.
Two ravens make a showy landing
on the rock behind me. Thick-billed.
Close. Each squawk, a detonation.
I get a little bothered, sandwiched
between the red-tail and the ravens, heads
like war hammers. Still, this privilege
of sudden beauty—and just when
I'd given up on mercy in the world.

FIRE SEASON WITH ROLLING BLACKOUTS AT THE BODEGA BAR & GRILL

After a week of enforced night,
light breaks over the pool table.
A clack of cues to crack the silence.
All that was perishable is gone
into two dumpsters out back. New,
on a whiteboard behind the bar,
these offerings: Pork belly, salmon,
short ribs, butterscotch pudding with
or without whipped cream. Also,
Everything is free
for fire survivors, first responders,
or anyone who needs it to be.

Generosity is a poem tonight,
the language of kindness to strangers
and gratitude to the volunteers
whose red engines screamed
from the firehouse next door.
No one will argue bumper stickers,
wonder who arrived with gun racks
or rainbow flags, attack a slogan
on someone's sweat-stained cap.
Just walking through the warped
doorway that never keeps the flies out
is a celebration of survival,

a free offer, a feast, a toast
to the shared citizenship of flesh.
Here's to the live and kicking,
those with hungers and with thirsts:
waitresses, barkeeps, cooks,
paying customers (or not),
praying customers (or not),
sooty cows in too-dry hills whose shit

sustains the flies. Here's to the frantic
flies, to all of us powerless
while flames choose what to burn
in this raging democracy of fire.

NOTES

"Canine"—In memory of Aleta Polk Watson.

"Bright Clutter"—In memory of Joshua Clayton Cohen.

"Green Burial"—In memory of Janice Berg Shulman. The epigraph is from advertising for Fernwood Cemetery in Mill Valley, California.

"Science News: Gene Tweak Can Extend Life 500% (But You Have to Be a Worm)"—The title includes a headline that appeared on the website *Live Science* on January 15, 2020.

"Science News: Snakes Had Back Legs for 70 Million Years, Fossil Record Says"—The title is a composite of headlines from multiple news sites in November, 2019.

"Science News: The Moisture in Fingerprints Strengthens Human Touch"—The title is a composite based on news stories that appeared in November, 2020.

"Report on the State of the World's Children"—UNICEF issues an annual report called The State of the World's Children. Data from the United Nations High Commissioner for Refugees showed that the global number of child refugees more than doubled between 2005 and 2020, even before more recent disasters.

"Photograph of Claudia Patricia Gómez González, Killed by U.S. Border Patrol Agent"—Inspired by a photograph that appeared with a news story in the *New York Times* on May 26, 2018.

"Another Alphabet"—Yiddish is the language of Central and Eastern European Jews and their descendants. It derived from High German in the early Middle Ages and includes words from Hebrew and Aramaic as well as from the various lands where Jewish populations lived over the past thousand years in Europe. Yiddish is written with the Hebrew alphabet or *Alef-beys*. Before World War II and the Holocaust, it had millions of speakers and a rich literary culture. *Rugelach* are crescent rolled cookies filled with raisins, walnuts, cinnamon, or other ingredients.

"Later, in America"—A *shul* can be either a school or synagogue. Here, I mean a school. *Klangen* means sounds, but can also refer to rumors. I like both definitions. *Shtetl* refers to small Eastern European towns with Jewish communities or to the communities themselves.

"Conversation Group in a Haunted Language"—Dedicated to Ben Stern, who survived two ghettos, nine concentration camps, and two death marches.

"Science News: As Animals and Plants Go Extinct, Languages Die Off Too"—The title includes a headline published in *VICE*, November 20, 2019.

"Science News: Dogs Were Domesticated Once from a Lost Population of Wolves"—The title includes a headline that appeared in *Ars Technica*, November 29, 2020.

"Science News: Dung Beetles Navigate by Storing Star Maps in their Brains"—Based on various headlines, including one in *Gizmodo* on May 13, 2016.

"Rosh Hashanah with Crow"—Rosh Hashanah, the Jewish new year, is celebrated by wishing people *l'shana tova*, which is Hebrew that means "for a good year." According to Jewish tradition, each year God inscribes the names of the righteous in the book of life. Apples and honey are a tradition meant to start the year off sweet.

"Breathing Fire from Paradise"—The Camp Fire in 2018 almost completely destroyed the town of Paradise, California, and killed at least 85 people. At the time, it was the most destructive and deadliest wildfire in state history. Smoke was visible from as far away as New York City and hazardous air choked Northern California for days.

"Science News: Amphibians Glow. Humans Just Couldn't See It—Until Now"—This title includes a headline from *WIRED*, February 27, 2020.

"Fire Season with Rolling Blackouts at the Bodega Bar & Grill"—Based on a sign that appeared in the tiny town of Bodega, California, north of San Francisco. The Pacific Gas & Electric Company shut down electricity for as long as a week in various communities in an attempt to prevent PG&E equipment from causing more wildfires.

Acknowledgments

American Journal of Poetry: "The Drill"

Atlanta Review: "Anniversary" (International Publication Award)

Catamaran Literary Reader: "In Greenland the Ice Sheet"

COMP; an interdisciplinary journal: "Just When," "Photograph of Claudia Patricia Gómez González, Killed by U.S. Border Patrol Agent"

Cutthroat, a Journal of the Arts: "Fire Season with Rolling Blackouts at the Bodega Bar & Grill" (2nd Prize Joy Harjo Poetry Award)

DMQ Review, disquieting muses quarterly: "Science News: Dogs Were Domesticated Once from a Lost Population of Wolves," "Science News: Dung Beetles Navigate by Storing Star Maps in their Brains"

Greensboro Review: "Weather Forecast"

Jabberwock Review: "They've Discovered the Spiders Can Hear Us"

JuxtaProse: "I Imagine Myself Grateful"

Los Angeles Review: "Bright Clutter"

Mudfish: "Conversation Group in a Haunted Language"

Nimrod International Journal: "Love in a Year of El Niño," "Green Burial," "A Dictionary Names the Wind in the Trees"

Northwest Review: "Science News: The Bubble Around the Universe Is Shaped Like a Collapsed Croissant"

PANK, Jewish Diaspora Folio: "Yiddish Cento," "Later, in America"

Poet Lore: "#sardiniansunday"

Portside: "Where Will You Go When Things Get Worse?"

Prairie Schooner: "Rosh Hashanah with Crow"

Red Wheelbarrow Literary Journal: "In Respect to the Jellyfish" (2021 Red Wheelbarrow Poetry Prize)

Southern Humanities Review: "Another Alphabet" (as "A Different Alphabet")

Southern Review: "Natural History"

Spillway: "Exhilaration"

Split Rock Review: "Omens Being Bad"

Tar River Poetry: "Report on the State of the World's Children," "Once," "Circuit of Sadness"

Terrain.org: "Science News: Snakes Had Back Legs for 70 Million Years, Fossil Record Says," "Science News: Gene Tweak Can Extend Life 500% (But You Have to Be a Worm)," "Science News: A Wild Bird Leads People to Honey," "Science News: Amphibians Glow. Humans Just Couldn't See It—Until Now," "Science News: As Animals and Plants Go Extinct, Languages Die Off Too" (Winner 11th Annual Poetry Contest)

32 Poems: "Hoop After Hoop"

Valparaiso Poetry Review: "Anthropometry"

West Trestle Review: "Canine"

These poems appeared first in anthologies:

America, We Call Your Name; Poems of Resistance and Rebellion (Sixteen Rivers Press; 2018): "Love in a Year of Outrage"
Marin Poetry Center Anthology 2019: "Muted"
Scientists and Poets #Resist (Brill; 2019): "Photosynthesis"

"Letter Home" was first published on the Tor House Foundation website, as an honorable mention in the 2018 Tor House Poetry Prize competition.

My gratitude also to the editors who reprinted these poems:

Canary: "In Greenland the Ice Sheet"
Rewilding; Poems for the Environment (Flexible Press; 2020): "Natural History" and "Where Will You Go When Things Get Worse?"
Why These Rocks; 50 Years of Poems from the Community of Writers (Heyday; 2021): "Natural History"

This book could not have been written without the feedback and encouragement of others. For some of the earliest poems, thank you to Lisa Allen Ortiz and Roy Mash. For most of this work, how fortunate I have been to be part of an extraordinary writing group: Susan Browne, Rebecca Foust, Julia Levine, and Jeanne Wagner. You all continue to amaze me with your talent.

A special gratitude to Jeanne Wagner, also, for more than fifteen years of close poetry friendship, and for comments and suggestions on the manuscript. To Cynthia Neely and Martha K. Grant who volunteered to cast their eyes on the final version, thank you.

Thank you to the judges who honored some of these poems in contests: Richard Blanco, Vievee Francis, Kimberly Blaeser, Arthur Sze, and Mark Doty.

To my fellow Yiddish speakers and learners, *a hartzikn dank* for embracing me as a beginner, sharing your knowledge, and extending your friendship. Your laughter has been the raft that kept me afloat, dear Mame-Loshn Mamas: Millie Chazin, Judy Kennedy, Colleen McKee, Sharon Pincus, Norma Solarz, and Dolores Taller.

To my family, as always. In particular, admiration as well as gratitude to my daughter Sarah Loyola for her cover art and to her husband Valentino Loyola for his photographic skills. To my husband for the support that makes long marriage worth writing about.

My deep appreciation to Broadstone Books, Larry W. Moore and Sheila Bucy Potter, who selected and published *Democracy of Fire*, for their love of the language of poetry.

Finally, of all the poets I've been lucky to know and who are now gone, I'd especially like to honor the memories of Chana Bloch and Marvin Bell. I call on both of them so often in my head that they are probably tired of hearing from me.

ABOUT THE AUTHOR

Susan Cohen is the author of two chapbooks and two previous full-length collections of poems, as well as co-author of a non-fiction book. She was a newspaper reporter, contributing writer to the *Washington Post Magazine*, and faculty member of the University of California Graduate School of Journalism before studying bioethics and poetry at Stanford University while on a John S. Knight fellowship for mid-career journalists. Her numerous journalism honors include a grant from the Fund for Investigative Reporting and two Science in Society Awards from the National Association of Science Writers. In 2013, she turned her full writing attention to poetry and earned an MFA from Pacific University. Her second full-length collection, *A Different Wakeful Animal*, won the 2015 David Martinson-Meadowhawk prize from Red Dragonfly Press and she's received recognition for many of her individual poems, including the Rita Dove Poetry Award from the Center for Women Writers, *Harpur Palate*'s Milton Kessler Memorial Poetry Prize, the Red Wheelbarrow Prize, and the Annual Poetry Prize from Terrain.org. Her work has appeared in the *Atlanta Review 25th Anniversary Anthology*, *Bloomsbury Anthology of Contemporary Jewish American Poetry*, *Los Angeles Review*, *Northwest Review*, *Prairie Schooner*, *Southern Humanities Review*, *Southern Review*, *Tar River Poetry*, *32 Poems*, and dozens of other publications. She lives in Berkeley, California.